FRIDA KAHLO

ARTIST AND ACTIVIST

FRIDA KAHLO

ARTIST AND ACTIVIST

MATT DOEDEN

LERNER PUBLICATIONS ◆ MINNEAPOLIS

Lerner Publications Company
An imprint of Lerner Publishing Group, Inc.
241 First Avenue North
Minneapolis, MN 55401 USA
For reading levels and more information, look up this title at www.lernerbooks.com.

Image credits: Bettmann/Getty Images, pp. 2, 13, 28, 34, 35, 39; Michael Ochs Archives/Getty Images, p. 6; Galerie Bilderwelty/Getty Images, pp. 9, 18; Guillermo Kahlo/Museo Frida Kahlo/Wikipedia Commons (PD), p. 10; Ángel Hernández/CDMX Secretariat of Culture, p. 12; Daniel Leal-Olivas/ AFP/Getty Images, p. 15; Elijah-Lovkoff/Getty Images, p. 16; Guillermo Kahlo/Sotheby's/Wikipedia PD (PD), p. 17; Fotosearch/Getty Images, p. 19; Fine Art Images/Heritage Images/Getty Images, p. 20; Andrew Hasson/Getty Images, p. 21; VCG Wilson/Getty Images, p. 23; Frida Kahlo (Mexican, 1907–1954). Self-Portrait Along the Border Line Between Mexico and the United States, 1932. © Banco de México Diego Rivera Frida Kahlo Museums Trust, Mexico, D.F./Artists Rights Society (ARS), New York.. Photograph by A. Burkatovski/Fine Art Images/SuperStock, p. 24; Hulton Archive/Getty Images, p. 26; Gamma-Keystone /Getty Images, p. 30; Frida Kahlo (Mexican, 1907–1954). The Two Fridas, 1939. © 2019 Banco de México Diego Rivera Frida Kahlo Museums Trust, Mexico City/Artists Rights Society (ARS), New York. Photograph by Luisa Ricciarini/Bridgeman Images; H. Armstrong Roberts/ClassicStock/Getty Images, p. 32; Lipnitzki/Roger Viollet/Getty Images, p. 33; Anton_Ivanov/ Shutterstock.com, p. 36; Valery Sharifulin\TASS/Getty Images, p. 37; Jeffrey Greenberg/Universal Images Group/Getty Images, p. 38; Ulises Ruiz/AFP/Getty Images, p. 40; Nathalie Speliers Ufermann/ Shutterstock.com, p. 41. Cover: Bettmann/Getty Images.
Illustrated design elements: Lauren Cooper/Independent Picture Service.

Main body text set in Rotis Serif Std. Typeface provided by Adobe Systems.

Library of Congress Cataloging-in-Publication Data

Names: Doeden, Matt, author.
Title: Frida Kahlo : artist and activist / Matt Doeden.
Description: Minneapolis : Lerner Publications, [2020] | Series: Gateway biographies | Includes
    bibliographical references and index. | Audience: Ages 9–14 | Audience: Grades 4–6 | Summary:
    "Mexican artist Frida Kahlo has become an icon for Chicanos as well as for the feminist and
    LGBTQ+ movements. Learn more about her life as an artist and political activist"– Provided by
    publisher.
Identifiers: LCCN 2019030030 (print) | LCCN 2019030031 (ebook) | ISBN 9781541577459 (library
    binding) | ISBN 9781541588882 (paperback) | ISBN 9781541583061 (ebook)
Subjects: LCSH: Kahlo, Frida–Juvenile literature. | Artists–Mexico–Biography–Juvenile literature. |
    Political activists–Mexico–Biography–Juvenile literature. | Women artists–Mexico–Biography–
    Juvenile literature. | Women political activists–Mexico–Biography–Juvenile literature.
Classification: LCC N6559.K34 D64 2020 (print) | LCC N6559.K34 (ebook) | DDC 700.92–dc23

LC record available at https://lccn.loc.gov/2019030030
LC ebook record available at https://lccn.loc.gov/2019030031

Manufactured in the United States of America
1-46768-47759-9/26/2019

CONTENTS

Kahlo posing for a portrait at the home and studio she shared with her husband, Diego Rivera

September 17, 1925, started out like any other day for eighteen-year-old Frida Kahlo. She took the bus to Mexico City to go to school. After class, she and her boyfriend, Alejandro Gómez Arias, were ready to leave the bustling city to return home to the nearby town of Coyoacán. The pair climbed aboard a wooden-bodied bus bound for home.

She had followed this routine countless times. But this day was different. Along the way, the bus driver accidentally crossed the path of a streetcar. The streetcar slammed into the side of the bus, pushing it along until it smashed into a wall. The wooden body of the bus splintered into pieces. People were thrown from the wreckage. Several died. Many more were wounded.

Gómez Arias was one of the lucky ones. He was thrown from the bus, but he suffered no serious injury. Dazed, he rushed to find Frida.

She had not been so lucky. Her body had been tossed, bent, and broken. A metal handrail had punctured her abdomen and pierced her uterus. Her right leg was shattered. Her spine was broken in three places. Her collarbone was broken as well.

Kahlo was in shock and confused. She didn't yet realize what had happened to her. Gómez Arias tried to pick her up, but she screamed in pain as he tried to move her. In the confusion, someone pulled the handrail from Frida's body. Her screams, Gómez Arias later said, were louder than the ambulance sirens.

Kahlo was rushed to a hospital. Her prospects were grim. She was in a fight for her life. And even though she survived her injuries, she was forever changed. In many ways, the accident marked the beginning of her journey to becoming one of Mexico's greatest artists. For the rest of her life, Kahlo would communicate her struggles with pain, both physical and emotional, through art.

CHILDHOOD IN COYOACÁN

Magdalena Carmen Frieda Kahlo y Calderón was born July 6, 1907, in Coyoacán, Mexico, near Mexico City. She preferred to go by Frida and used this spelling of her name for much of her life. She was the third of four daughters born to Guillermo Kahlo and Matilde Calderón y González. Frida also had two half sisters from her father's first marriage, but Frida's mother would not allow them to live with the family. Instead, they lived in an orphanage.

Frida grew up in Casa Azul, a house that her father built. Her family was diverse. Her mother was half Spanish and half indigenous Mexican. Her father had immigrated to Mexico from Germany. It was not always a happy home. Frida's parents were often ill, and they did not seem to enjoy each other's company. Frida's mother was very strict, and the two of them did not get along well. Frida's relationship with her father, a photographer, was much warmer. Frida spent much of her time in the village and the countryside exploring, visiting markets, and spending time with friends.

When Frida was six, she became ill with polio. The serious and sometimes deadly disease often left survivors disabled for life. She spent nine months in bed recovering. The disease

Frida's father changed his name from Wilhelm to Guillermo when he immigrated to Mexico.

left her with a deformed and weak right leg. Her doctors recommended exercise to strengthen the leg, so her father made Frida swim and ride a bike.

Frida poses for a portrait on June 15, 1919.

It was an unhappy time for Frida. The other children made fun of her, calling her Pata de Palo, Spanish for "Wooden Leg" or "Peg Leg." She was deeply self-conscious of her leg, both as a child and through adulthood. She was lonely. She later recalled inventing an imaginary playmate for herself. She would blow on a window and then draw a door where her breath had condensed. She

imagined running through the door into an imaginary world where she would meet her friend.

Frida's father helped her get through what was at times a difficult childhood. At the time, most women in Mexico took on traditional roles of keeping house and raising a family. But he wanted his daughter to have options. He shared his love of art and photography with her. He taught her how to take photographs, as well as how to retouch and color prints. Frida enjoyed being with her father, but she did not share his love of photography. She preferred to draw. One of his friends gave her drawing lessons. It sparked a love of art that would help to define Frida's life.

As Frida recovered from polio, she became her father's caretaker. He had epilepsy, with frequent and often violent seizures that would leave him unconscious. Often, as he awoke from his seizures, Frida was there by his side. Her father endured his condition with quiet dignity, a demeanor that Frida would adopt for herself later in life.

Frida was a curious and creative child with a bright mind and strong opinions. As she grew older, Frida excelled in school. In 1922, at the age of fifteen, she

enrolled at the Escuela Nacional Preparatoria in Mexico City. She had plans to go on to medical school to become a doctor. She thrived at the school despite being just one of a handful of girls admitted. She quickly made friends with some of her classmates, forming a group that they called the Cachuchas. They discussed current events, literature, and politics. They were deeply interested in the politics of socialism, where the government and people share the creation and distribution of goods, and communism, where a nation's property and goods are shared among all people. Kahlo became a devout supporter of communism and worked for the rest of her life to spread its message.

The Cachuchas weren't serious all the time, though. They pulled pranks, including setting off firecrackers during classes that they considered boring. It was a happy time for Frida. She felt welcomed and accepted.

During Frida's time at the school, famous Mexican artist Diego Rivera was painting one of his murals, *Creation*, in the school's courtyard. Sixteen-year-old Frida was enchanted with Rivera. She often shadowed the legendary painter, watching him work. She left an impression on the artist. He later wrote, "She had unusual dignity and self-assurance, and there was a strange fire in her eyes."

Frida had always been a free thinker, but at her new school, she became a true rebel. She adopted a style of her own, often dressing in men's clothing. She spent much of her time with her fellow group members, including Alejandro Gómez Arias, one of Frida's first loves.

Diego Rivera was already a world-famous artist by the time he painted the mural at Frida's school.

They loved to debate each other and discuss philosophy. So, it's no surprise Frida was with Gómez Arias on September 17, 1925, when she boarded the bus for a ride that would change her life forever.

DEATH DANCES

As Kahlo lay in the hospital after her accident, no one was sure whether she would live or die. She endured a series of painful surgeries, and she struggled to survive. "In this hospital, death dances around my bed at night," she told Gómez Arias.

STRETCHING THE TRUTH

Kahlo's creativity is a big part of what made her a great artist. But it didn't end with her art. Kahlo often gave creative—and untrue—accounts of her life. For example, she liked to tell people that she was born in 1910, the first year of the Mexican Revolution (1910–1920). She also claimed that her mother couldn't read, which wasn't true.

She stretched the truth about other aspects of her life, including her health, her upbringing, and her accident. For Kahlo, telling a good story was sometimes more important than telling the true story.

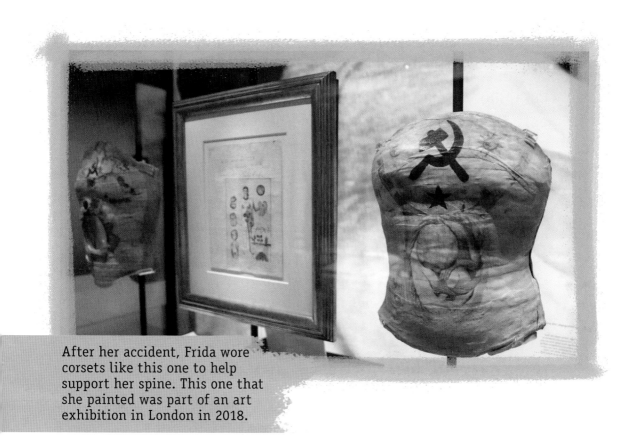

After her accident, Frida wore corsets like this one to help support her spine. This one that she painted was part of an art exhibition in London in 2018.

Slowly, Kahlo recovered. She had to wear a special garment called a corset to support her shattered spine. She spent three months in bed. She couldn't go to school, and her dreams of becoming a doctor faded away. Meanwhile, Gómez Arias's parents sent him to Germany to continue his studies. With an ocean between them, their relationship quickly ended. Losing Gómez Arias weighed heavily on Kahlo's mind. She fell into a depression.

"When you come [home] I won't be able to offer you anything you'd want," Kahlo wrote Gómez Arias in an anguished letter. "All of life is in you, but I can't have it. . . . I'm very foolish and suffering more than I should.

I'm quite young and it is possible for me to be healed, only I can't believe it; I shouldn't believe it, should I?"

Everything that had been important to Kahlo was gone—her education, her future plans, and her love. So her mind shifted back to art. She'd always been an artist. She casually drew sketches and had spent time working for an engraver. But she'd never seriously considered art as a career. As she lay in bed, unable to do much of anything else, art took on a new importance in her life. Her mother set up an easel beside her bed and positioned a mirror so that Frida could use her own reflection as a model.

Kahlo spent her days painting. She painted herself. She painted friends, family members, and visitors. She painted

Some of Kahlo's early paintings were inspired by her hometown of Coyoacán.

scenes from around Coyoacán. When she wasn't painting, she was often drawing.

As Kahlo continued to paint, her craft improved. Soon she wasn't simply painting for herself. Others wanted her paintings. Still, she did not see painting as a way to earn income. She gave her paintings away as gifts, often adding the name of the person who would receive it to the painting itself.

Kahlo poses for a photo taken by her father.

One painting in particular would help to shape Kahlo's future career. It was a portrait of herself, titled *Self-Portrait with Velvet Dress.* She portrayed herself with a very long, swanlike neck and long fingers. She painted it for Gómez Arias in 1926, possibly with the hope of winning back his love. The self-portrait, which she called a reflection, would become the style for which she would be most famous. Through her reflections, Kahlo appeared to look at the world from behind her own eyes.

NEW LOVE, NEW LIFE

Over the next few years, Kahlo continued to recover. She kept painting, often focusing on portraits of friends and family members. By 1928 she was able to leave her bed and return to the wider world. She had always loved exploring the countryside near her home, as well as the bustling streets of Mexico City. She began doing so again, but this time with an artist's eye. She threw herself into the artistic community. She also renewed her interest in socialism and communism. She spent her days discussing and debating art and politics. Her social group revolved around American photographer Tina Modotti, who shared many of Kahlo's beliefs and passions. The two became close friends.

Tina Modotti photographed the Mexican muralist movement in the 1920s.

Five years after they first met, Kahlo and Rivera began a whirlwind romance.

Meanwhile, Kahlo reconnected with someone from her past. In 1928, possibly at one of Modotti's parties, Kahlo once again met Diego Rivera, the muralist whom she had met when she was just sixteen years old. Rivera was a major figure in the art community and was an outspoken supporter of communism. Not surprisingly, Kahlo was drawn to him.

The pair hit it off and began a romance. They were an unlikely couple. Rivera was twenty-one years older than Kahlo was. He was a towering figure, weighing more than 300 pounds (136 kg). Frida, meanwhile, was a very small woman, weighing just 98 pounds (44 kg). Rivera would visit Kahlo at Casa Azul, where Kahlo would show him her paintings, and he would give her his criticism. "It was obvious to me that this girl was an authentic artist," he later wrote.

Kahlo's mother did not approve of the age difference between the two artists, nor of Rivera's atheism. But her father supported the match. Rivera was an accomplished artist who could provide for Kahlo, who still needed expensive medical treatment. He warned Rivera that life with his daughter would not be easy. But that didn't discourage Rivera. The romance moved swiftly, and the couple married on August 21, 1929. Kahlo's marriage to the famous muralist made her something of an overnight celebrity. Newspapers in Mexico, the United States, and Europe covered the couple's wedding.

Kahlo's father was supportive of her relationship with Rivera. Her mother did not approve.

The newly married couple moved to Cuernavaca, about 54 miles (87 km) south of Mexico City. Rivera had been hired to paint murals at the city's Palace of Cortés. While Rivera worked, Kahlo took in the Tehuana culture of the area. She loved it. She began to dress in traditional Tehuana style, with bright floral-patterned skirts and lace headdresses. Years later, she would paint one of her reflections, nicknamed *Diego on My Mind*, of herself wearing a traditional lace bridal outfit in the Tehuana style.

Several of Kahlo's Tehuana-inspired outfits are on display at the Frida Kahlo Museum in Mexico City.

While in Cuernavaca, the couple attempted to start a family. But Kahlo was unable to carry a child, probably because of the injuries to her uterus during her bus accident in 1925. She endured the first of several miscarriages, which sent her into a deep depression. The miscarriages cast a dark cloud over what was otherwise a happy time in her life.

DARK DAYS, DARK REFLECTIONS

After more than a year in Cuernavaca, Kahlo and Rivera were ready for a new adventure. In November 1930, the couple headed north to the United States. They settled in San Francisco, California, a city with an energetic art community. Rivera painted murals for the City Club of San Francisco and the California School of Fine Arts. Meanwhile, Kahlo continued her own artistic pursuits. She mainly painted portraits, many of which were self-portraits. She painted so many of them, she said, because she was so often alone. At this stage in her life, Kahlo was a talented artist but still an amateur. She was known more for being the wife of Diego Rivera than for her own work. She would watch her husband paint. She learned his techniques and applied them to her own art. With each passing year, her skills grew.

From California, the couple moved to New York City and Detroit, Michigan. Rivera loved life in the United States, where he was treated as a celebrity and a pillar of the art community. But Kahlo did not. She felt out of place. As a supporter of communism, she disliked the capitalist society that flourished in the United States. The rich lived a lavish life of luxury while the poor struggled just to eat each day. It went against everything she believed in as a Communist. Kahlo, who always had strong opinions, was not shy in her criticism. "I find that Americans completely lack sensibility and good taste," she said. "They are boring and they all have faces like unbaked rolls."

Kahlo disliked New York City. She thought it was too urban and industrial.

Self-Portrait on the Borderline between Mexico and the United States

Kahlo was desperately lonely and homesick. In 1932 those emotions came out in a reflection titled *Self-Portrait on the Borderline between Mexico and the United States.* The painting shows Kahlo standing between Mexico and the United States. Mexico, on the left, is a beautiful landscape with plants, blooming flowers, ancient ruins, the sun, and the moon. The United States, to the right, stands in stark contrast. It is urban and industrial. Smoke pours out of a factory, casting a cloud over the US flag. The ground is filled with wires instead of plant roots. The message is clear. Kahlo was miserable in the United States. She wanted to return home to Mexico.

Kahlo's mood darkened further after she suffered another miscarriage, and complications left her hospitalized for two weeks. She expressed her feelings about this time in her painting *Henry Ford Hospital.* In the painting, Kahlo lies naked and bleeding on a hospital bed. Six objects surround her, including the fetus of her unborn child. Some believe that this painting marked the beginning of Kahlo's defining style, in which she

SURREALISM

Many art historians and critics consider Kahlo's work to be surrealism. This style rose to popularity in the 1920s, just as Kahlo was coming into her own as an artist. Surrealist art features real objects and people in bizarre or illogical scenes. It has a dreamlike quality that often focuses on surprising or seemingly out-of-place elements.

The elements in surrealist work often serve as symbols or metaphors. For example, in Kahlo's famous painting *Henry Ford Hospital,* a wilted orchid seems to symbolize Kahlo's own damaged uterus and inability to have children.

However, Kahlo did not embrace the label of surrealist. "They thought I was a surrealist, but I wasn't," she said. "I never painted dreams. I painted my own reality."

lays her own pain bare on the canvas. For Kahlo, bad news just kept coming. A few months after her miscarriage, Kahlo's mother died.

After a brief return to Mexico, the couple went back to New York in 1933. Rivera worked on a mural for the Rockefeller Center. He loved his life as a celebrity in New York and desperately wanted to stay. Kahlo just as desperately wanted to go home to Mexico. During her time in New York, Kahlo threw all of her creative energy into a single painting, *My Dress Hangs There.*

The painting was an expression of the growing conflict between Kahlo and Rivera. It was unusual in that it was not a portrait. Kahlo's face does not appear in the painting—only her dress. The painting shows the United States in its industrial glory. Yet the scene is wrapped in chaos and decay. It's falling apart. It's a clear message about what Kahlo thought of American values and its capitalist ideals.

ARTIST AND ACTIVIST

Kahlo and Rivera returned to Mexico City in late 1933. Both were unhappy. Rivera's mural at Rockefeller Center had been destroyed because of its pro-Communist message. Kahlo felt that Rivera resented her for forcing him to return to Mexico. The couple began to drift apart. Kahlo was frequently ill and spent time in the hospital, possibly due to the stress in the marriage. The couple tried to make it work.

During the 1930s, Mexico City's area and population grew rapidly.

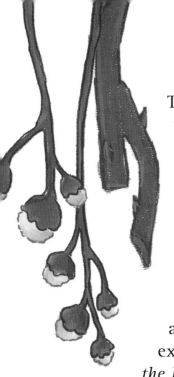

They moved into a new house in Mexico City, which included a studio for Kahlo. But it was not a productive time in her career, and she painted little.

Around this time, Rivera began an affair with Kahlo's younger sister, Cristina Kahlo. It had always been a loose bond between husband and wife, and both had taken on relationships outside of the marriage in the past. But the idea of Rivera with her sister added further emotional strain on Kahlo. She expressed her heartbreak in a painting, *Memory, the Heart* (1937). It shows her standing next to two dresses. One is the small dress of a schoolgirl. The second is a traditional Tehuana dress. Kahlo's heart lies at her feet, pumping blood onto the ground. The portrait may represent Kahlo's conflict over the differences between her childhood dreams and expectations, contrasted with the realities of her adult life.

It was a time of political turmoil in Mexico, and Rivera and Kahlo were right in the thick of it. In 1936 Kahlo joined a Socialist organization called the Fourth International, whose goal was to overthrow capitalism. She became a follower of Leon Trotsky, a Communist revolutionary in the Soviet Union (a group of republics that included Russia). He opposed the dictator Josef Stalin. The Soviet Union had exiled Trotsky, or kicked him out, for his views.

In 1937 Kahlo and Rivera convinced the Mexican government to allow the exiled Trotsky into Mexico. For the next two years, Trotsky lived at Casa Azul. Kahlo and Trotsky soon began a brief affair. She called him El Viejo, "The Old Man," and painted *Self-Portrait Dedicated to Leon Trotsky* for him. Unlike much of her work, this painting did not show the pain of Kahlo's life. Instead, it shows her in warm, soft colors, standing beneath billowing white curtains. In her hand she holds a note that reads, "To Leon Trotsky with all my love, I dedicate this painting [on] the 7th November 1937. Frida Kahlo. In Saint Angel, Mexico."

The two years that Trotsky spent in Casa Azul were highly productive for Kahlo. She continued to hone her craft, and her technical skills were growing. In 1938 actor and art collector Edward G. Robinson bought several of

Kahlo (*second from left*) welcomes Leon Trotsky (*second from right*) to Mexico in January 1937.

her paintings. Until that point, Kahlo had given away most of her work as gifts. The idea that she could make a living at painting filled her with joy. Knowing she could generate her own income was liberating. "For me it was such a surprise that I marveled and said: 'This way I am going to be able to be free, I'll be able to travel and do what I want without asking Diego for money.'"

That year Kahlo traveled to New York to show her work at the Julien Levy Gallery, which promoted surrealist art. Being the subject of an entire exhibition was a major step forward in Kahlo's career. The show was a success. She sold a number of paintings, and the show received rave reviews in *Time*, one of the most influential magazines of the day: "The flutter of the week in Manhattan was caused by the first exhibition of paintings by famed muralist Diego Rivera's . . . wife, Frida Kahlo. . . . Frida's pictures, mostly painted in oil on copper, had the daintiness of miniatures, the vivid reds and yellows of Mexican tradition, the playfully bloody fancy of an unsentimental child."

As Kahlo's career was on the rise, her marriage was rockier than ever. In 1939 Kahlo and Rivera agreed to divorce. They remained friendly after their separation.

Kahlo and Rivera's marriage came to an end just as Kahlo's art began to receive worldwide recognition.

GROWING STATURE

Kahlo returned to Casa Azul in 1939. She had shown herself that she could make a living as a painter. She devoted herself to painting and began what may have been the most productive period of her life. She began painting larger works suitable for exhibitions. Over the next few years, Kahlo created a flurry of stunning works, including many of the paintings for which she is most famous.

In 1939 Kahlo painted *The Two Fridas*. It shows two seated images of herself, holding hands. The Frida on the left is dressed in a modern European style. This Frida is attempting to stem the blood from her broken heart using the clamp held in her right hand. The Frida of the right is wearing traditional Tehuana clothing. Her heart appears to be intact. Kahlo later said that the painting represented two aspects of her personality and her sadness as she came to terms with her divorce.

The Two Fridas

A year later, she painted *Self-Portrait with Thorn Necklace and Hummingbird*. In this striking reflection, Kahlo sits between a monkey and a panther. A thorn necklace adorned with a hummingbird sits around her neck. The thorns cause her neck to bleed, but her face shows no sign of pain. The imagery may have meant that Kahlo endured much of her pain without showing it to the world.

These were just a few of the memorable works Kahlo painted during this period. As she continued to work, Kahlo's reputation in the art community was steadily growing. In 1939 the Louvre Museum in Paris, France, purchased her painting *The Frame.* The purchase made her the first Mexican artist featured in the world's most famous art museum. The painting was experimental, with part of the painting done on an aluminum sheet and the rest on a sheet of glass that lays over the top of it.

The Louvre is the world's largest art museum.

Kahlo had carved out her own place in the art world, shedding the label of Diego Rivera's wife. She traveled to Europe, where she met legendary artist Pablo Picasso. He was a fan of her work and gave her a pair of earrings in the shape of hands as a gift. Kahlo wore the earrings in her 1940 painting, *Self-Portrait, Dedicated to Dr Eloesser.*

LIVING IN PAIN

Despite her growing success, Kahlo's life was in turmoil. In 1940 Trotsky was assassinated in Coyoacán. Kahlo, briefly a suspect in the murder, was cleared of any involvement. Later that year, Kahlo and Rivera remarried. They lived together at Casa Azul but agreed to an open marriage in which both could see other people.

Pablo Picasso was a Spanish artist who spent much of his life in France.

Kahlo and Rivera sign their marriage certificate after divorcing a year earlier.

Meanwhile, Kahlo's health was in sharp decline. She suffered terrible pain from the breaks in her spine, which had never fully healed. Her legs gave her pain, and an infection in her hand proved difficult to cure. The stress from her father's death in 1941 made her health problems worse. In 1943 Kahlo accepted a teaching position at La Esmeralda, a school of fine arts. But it was a short-lived position, as her health forced her to remain home.

As she always had, Kahlo expressed her pain through her art. In 1944 she painted *The Broken Column*. It shows her partly nude, standing in a desolate field with nails piercing her body. Her abdomen and chest are split open, revealing a broken column where her spine should have been. A corset appears to be all that's holding her body together. It was a clear message that Kahlo felt her own health slipping away.

The theme of pain dominated her work of this period. Her 1945 painting *Without Hope* shows her lying in bed, being force-fed a vile mixture of meat and bone through a funnel. The painting shows the helplessness Kahlo must have been feeling. On the back of the painting, she wrote, "Not the least hope remains to me."

Over the next several years, Kahlo underwent a series of surgeries. Among them was a spinal surgery in 1946. Doctors tried to rebuild her spine using bone and steel. It was a failure. The pain continued, making it difficult for Kahlo to sit or stand. Dealing with constant pain, Kahlo became addicted to both alcohol and painkillers. The

Despite several surgeries, Kahlo continued to struggle with pain.

quality of her work began to diminish. She continued to show her paintings despite her poor health, even arriving at one exhibition in an ambulance. But many art critics agreed that her greatest work was behind her.

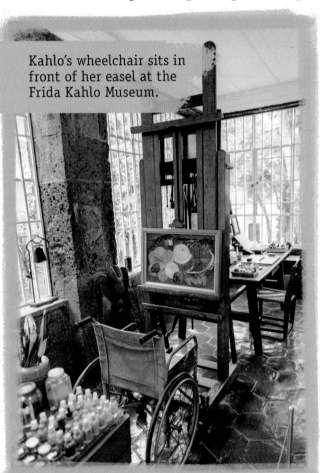

Kahlo's wheelchair sits in front of her easel at the Frida Kahlo Museum.

KAHLO'S FINAL YEARS

Kahlo's ailments dominated her final years. In 1950 doctors attempted once again to fix her spine. The surgery resulted in an infection that required several more surgeries to correct. When she finally did leave the hospital, she needed crutches and a

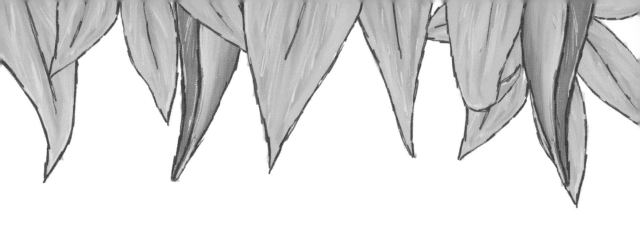

wheelchair. In 1951 she painted *Self-Portrait with the Portrait of Doctor Farill*. It showed her in her wheelchair next to a portrait of her doctor. Kahlo holds paintbrushes and a palette in the shape of her own heart. It was the last signed self-portrait Kahlo would ever paint.

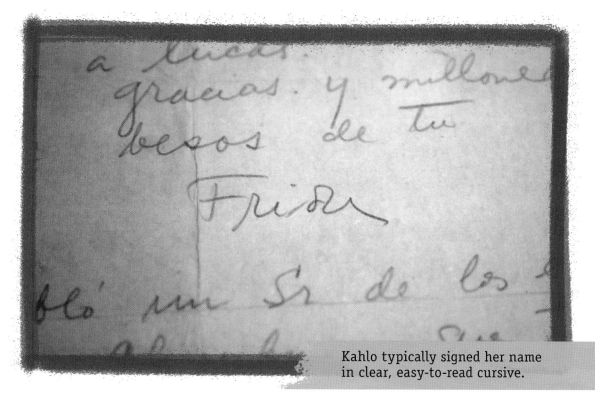

Kahlo typically signed her name in clear, easy-to-read cursive.

Meanwhile, Kahlo remained devoted to politics. She renewed her support for communism and campaigned for world peace. She painted portraits of Communist leaders such as Karl Marx and Josef Stalin. Yet her health and addictions continued to weigh her down. In 1953 gangrene forced doctors to amputate her infected right leg at the knee. Kahlo fell into a deep depression.

Kahlo wore this prosthetic after her right leg was amputated in 1953.

In July 1954, Kahlo attended a political demonstration—her final public appearance. A few days later, on the morning of July 13, a nurse found Kahlo dead in her bed. She was forty-seven years old.

The following day, friends and family attended a small ceremony while more than six hundred admirers stood by outside, mourning her loss. Kahlo had dreaded being buried, so she was cremated. Her ashes were returned in a ceramic urn to Casa Azul. Rivera was distraught, and many close to him believe that he never recovered from Kahlo's death. He died just three years later.

Friends and family attended Kahlo's funeral service. Hundreds of her admirers stood outside.

A GROWING LEGACY

Kahlo spent much of her career unknown to the art world. Her early fame came largely from her marriage to Diego Rivera. In her mid-thirties, she gained attention on the merit of her work.

However, Kahlo's stature in the art world continued to grow after her death. In 1958 Casa Azul was converted into a museum in Kahlo's honor. In the 1970s, feminist movements rediscovered and spread appreciation of Kahlo's work. In 1984 Mexico declared her paintings to be

Fin Dac's mural *Magdalena* in Guadalajara, Mexico, honors Kahlo.

works of national cultural heritage and banned their exportation. The ban created a sudden scarcity of available paintings, putting her work in higher demand than ever before. In 2016 her 1939 painting *Two Nudes in the Forest* sold at an auction for a stunning $8 million.

Kahlo has also become a part of popular culture. Her style has inspired fashion designers. In 2002 actor Salma Hayek starred in a biopic about the artist, titled *Frida*. The film was a hit with critics. Nominated for six Academy Awards, it won for Best Makeup and Best Original Score. Kahlo was also a character in Disney's 2017 animated film *Coco*.

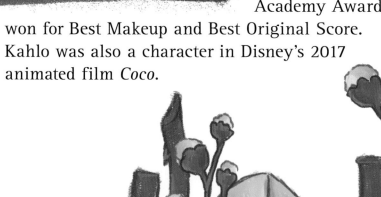

Kahlo is featured on the
Mexican 500-peso bill.

Kahlo didn't plan to be an artist. A tragic accident sent her down a path she had never intended to follow. But her pain, and her ability to translate it into her art, has made her one of the most beloved artists of the twentieth century. More than sixty years after her death, she continues to inspire and move people with her art and her story of overcoming adversity.

41

IMPORTANT DATES

1907   Frida Kahlo is born July 6 in Coyoacán, Mexico.

1922   At the age of fifteen, Frida enrolls at Escuela Nacional Preparatoria in Mexico City.

1925   A terrible bus accident leaves Kahlo wounded and near death.

1926   Kahlo paints *Self Portrait with Velvet Dress* as a gift for Alejandro Gómez Arias.

1928   Kahlo meets famous muralist Diego Rivera for the second time at a party. They begin a courtship.

1929   Kahlo and Rivera marry and move to Cuernavaca.

1930   Kahlo and Rivera move to the United States, first living in San Francisco, California.

1932   Kahlo begins to develop her signature style in paintings such as *Henry Ford Hospital* and *Self-Portrait on the Borderline between Mexico and the United States.*

1933   Kahlo and Rivera return to Mexico.

1937   Russian revolutionary Leon Trotsky lives in exile in
             Kahlo's childhood home. The two begin a brief affair.

1938   Kahlo's work is shown at an exhibition in New York City.

1939   Kahlo and Rivera divorce. Kahlo paints *The Two Fridas* to
             show her distress over the split.

1946   A failed spinal surgery leaves Kahlo in terrible pain. She
             expresses her mood in the painting *Without Hope*.

1950   Kahlo endures a series of surgeries on her back and
             spends months in the hospital.

1953   Doctors amputate part of Kahlo's right leg.

1954   Kahlo dies on July 13 at the age of forty-seven.

SOURCE NOTES

13 Phyllis Tuchman, "Frida Kahlo," *Smithsonian Magazine*, November 2002, https://www.smithsonianmag.com/arts-culture /frida-kahlo-70745811/.

14 Tuchman.

15–16 Gerry Souter, *Frida Kahlo: Beneath the Mirror* (New York: Parkstone, 2005), 25.

19 Tuchman, "Frida Kahlo."

23 Tuchman.

25 "Frida Kahlo and Surrealism," FridaKahlo.org, accessed June 25, 2019, https://www.fridakahlo.org/link.jsp.

28 *Self-Portrait Dedicated to Leon Trotsky*, FridaKahlo.org, accessed June 25, 2019, https://www.fridakahlo.org/self-portrait -dedicated-to-leon-trotsky.jsp.

29 Tuchman, "Frida Kahlo."

29 Tuchman.

35 *Without Hope*, FridaKahlo.org, accessed June 25, 2019, https:// www.fridakahlo.org/without-hope.jsp.

SELECTED BIBLIOGRAPHY

Ankori, Gannit. *Frida Kahlo*. London: Reaktion Books, 2013.

"Frida Kahlo and Her Paintings." FridaKahlo.org. Accessed May 21, 2019. http://FridaKahlo.org.

Souter, Gerry. *Frida Kahlo: Beneath the Mirror*. New York: Parkstone, 2005.

Tibol, Raquel. *Frida Kahlo: An Open Life*. Albuquerque: University of New Mexico Press, 1993. https://www.biography.com/news/frida -kahlo-bus-accident.

Tuchman, Phyllis. "Frida Kahlo." *Smithsonian Magazine*, November 2002. https://www.smithsonianmag.com/arts-culture/frida-kahlo -70745811/?page=2.

FURTHER READING

Ducksters: Surrealism Art for Kids
https://www.ducksters.com/history/art/surrealism.php
What is surrealism? When did it start? Who are some famous
surrealists? Find the answers at Ducksters.

Kay, Ann. *Art and How It Works: An Introduction to Art for Children.*
New York: DK, 2018.
Take a colorful journey through the history of art from cave
paintings and Renaissance art to modern graffiti. Find out how and
why art is made.

Medina, Mariana, and Sara McIntosh Wooten. *Frida Kahlo: Self-Portrait
Artist.* New York: Enslow, 2016.
Learn more about Kahlo's life, her struggles with her health, and the
art that made her famous.

Red Ted Art: Frida Kahlo Projects for Kids
https://www.redtedart.com/frida-kahlo-projects-for-kids/
See some of Kahlo's artwork, learn about her life, and practice your
own Kahlo-inspired art.

Reef, Catherine. *Frida & Diego: Art, Love, Life.* Boston: Houghton Mifflin
Harcourt, 2014.
Read more about the often-rocky love affair between two of
Mexico's greatest artists.

INDEX